I0159455

# Apprecative Inquiry

## 90 Minute Guides

Written by: Michelle N. Halsey, PMP

Silver City Publications & Training, L.L.C.

# COPYRIGHT

Copyright© 2016 Silver City Publication & Training, L.L.C.

Author: Michelle N. Halsey

ISBN: 978-1-64004-003-8

Silver City Publications and Training, L.L.C.

PO Box 1914

Nampa, ID 83653

https://www.silvercitypublications.com/shop/

# TABLE OF CONTENTS

# Chapter 1 – Getting Started

Appreciative inquiry focuses on finding the best in people and how they use it to function in their work and everyday life. Through appreciative inquiry, an employer uses the art of asking questions and opinions to strengthen the system as a whole, creating a more positive environment and heightening employee potential. This approach is designed to focus less on negativity and criticism, and utilize personal design and encourage discovery.

Research has consistently demonstrated that when clear goals are associated with learning, it occurs more easily and rapidly. With that in mind, let's review our goals.

At the end of this tutorial, participants should be able to:

- Know the meaning of appreciative inquiry

- Think in positive terms and avoid thinking negatively

- Encourage others to think positively

- Recognize positive attributes in people

- Create positive imagery

- Manage and guide employees in a positive environment

## Before you start:

On a sheet of paper, make note of what you hope to learn or goals you want to accomplish from this study guide.

1. What does Appreciative Inquiry mean to you?

2. What do you hope to learn from this study guide?

3. How can this class help you at your job?

4. How can appreciative inquiry help you achieve your career goals?

5. Any other thoughts?

# Chapter 2 – Introducing Appreciative Inquiry

Before someone can begin to utilize appreciative inquiry, they must first know what it is and what it means. There are many techniques and practices that can be used with appreciative inquiry that anyone can use in their lives. Learning about appreciative inquiry not only benefits the employee, but the entire company. It helps address ways to encourage positive ways of thinking instead of using negativity or even criticism.

## What is Appreciative Inquiry?

The definition of appreciative inquiry is the ability to recognize the best in people and utilizing those strengths to discover new possibilities and results. Appreciative inquiry focuses on positive thinking and expresses ideas and opinions to reach an end result. What does that mean for you or your business? Appreciative inquiry in the workplace encourages employees to think positively, which in turn helps them to overcome their own negative thoughts to work harder and reach their own goals for better productivity.

## Generating a Better Future

Appreciative inquiry helps build a vision for a better future by using questions to turn the person's attention to their past, present and future successes. These questions generally focus on what the person enjoys about their surroundings and their current situations. Once these ideas have been identified, the individual can take these positive thoughts to turn toward the future and build a path to success. Since we, as people, learn from our past mistakes and choices, we can use questions and insights to decide what we can use to make the right choices later. The key is identifying what works for you, and how you can use them to your advantage to create a better future.

Ways to create your future today:

- Determine your goals

- Make a plan for them

- Identify how appreciative inquiry can affect these goals and plans

### Creating My Better Future Exercise

There are different ways you begin to create your better future today. Decide on a few plans that you would use and plan how to implement them. On a piece of paper, write down a list of 3 to 5 goals you want to achieve. For each goal, brainstorm a list of activities that will help form these goals. Finally, develop ways to execute the ideas into a plan.

## Engaging People in Positive Thought

One of the age-old ways of determining how a person views a situation is asking them if the glass is half full or half empty. Many pessimists will reply that the glass is half empty while opportunists will see the glass as half full. Even one pessimist in the group can hinder everyone else's positive attitude, so it is important to engage every employee in positive thinking. When everyone avoids criticism and implements the '*can do attitude*', it not only creates a pleasant work environment for everyone, but employees begin to feel better about themselves and take pride to finish any job with ease.

Engaging others to think positive:

Encourage group discussions

Invite others to share their ideas and opinions

Make them focus on the positive side of things and avoid negative phrasings

Think of areas you could think more positively.  List something you can do to that goal. Determine what can you do to achieve your goals?

# Change the Person, Change the Organization

When employees take pride in themselves, they also take pride in their company.  But if they have negative feelings about where they work, it can show in their productivity. When you change how a person views or thinks about the company and their roles in it, you in turn change how the company is perceived as a whole. This is why it is always important to meet with employees and listen to what they have to say; value their ideas and opinions.

If the employee feels as though they are making a contribution to the company and are a part of the master plan, they will feel more inclined to think positively and alter the overall view of the organization. With positive and reflective employees the organization should then become a positive entity and provide a better environment for everyone.

# Case Study

Alex and Marshall are doing some brainstorming on marketing ideas for a new project. They were stuck on forming new ideas, so Alex decided to use Appreciative Inquiry to see if it could help them along. He told Marshall that they are making changes for the future and wanted him to feel confident in his efforts. He asked Marshall for his opinions on the new product and what he thought about it.

Marshall was instantly intrigued and began talking more about the product and what he thought about it. He opened up with positive thoughts and soon had lots of new ideas. Alex was glad that Marshall could open up more and share his ideas because he knew it would help them do a great job for the company.

# Chapter 3 – Changing the Way You Think

One of the simplest ways to relieve stress and feel better about ourselves is to change the way we think about things in our lives. Having a positive attitude allows a person to change their own lives because it shows that they have an understanding of their surroundings and feel confident enough to use them to their advantage. But if we hide behind negative thoughts and allow our environment to make us sad or depressed, we may never have the drive to reach for our goals and ambitions.

## Shifting from "What's Wrong?" to "What's Right?"

One of the first things that can ruin a positive attitude is looking at a situation and only noticing the negative aspects, or the "What's Wrong" side. Since the main focus of appreciative inquiry is being positive and aiming towards goals, a pessimistic attitude won't get anyone very far. When presented with a problem, take a few minutes and look at both sides of the problem. Make a mental list of everything that is positive about the situation before touching on the negative aspects. You'll find that any situation won't appear as bad as we think when we notice the positive first.

Keys to shifting our thoughts:

Avoid the "all or nothing" thinking – deciding a situation only has two sides.

Realize the difference between being right and being happy.

Avoid over-generalizing a situation – focus on details.

Wrong vs. Right Exercise

Sometime we can look at a situation as wrong or right. Sometimes we find similarities in each situation we come across. Think about your current job position. What do you find wrong with it? What do you find right with it? Take some time to write down what is wrong and what is right. After you write down what is wrong and right, what key elements can you identify in each set of situations?

## It's Not Eliminating Mistakes-It's Holding up Successes

A common misconception that people make is that being positive or progressive means they cannot make mistakes nor have faults. This, of course, is untrue. Mistakes happen all the time, and although they can sometimes be prevented, they cannot be stopped altogether. The key is to learn from your mistakes and then focus on the successes that follow them.

When a child falls off their bike before learning to ride, we do not focus on how many times they fell, but celebrate when they ride down the sidewalk on their own. Being positive doesn't mean we eliminate mistakes or problems, we just learn to focus on the achievements we reach. Success leads to more success when we are focused on the positive.

## Positive Language Will Affect People's Thinking

From a young age we have learned that positive language has more effect on us than negativity. When we tell ourselves "*I can't do that*" or "*I'll never finish this*", we normally find ourselves to be right. But if we use more positive and influential phrases and language, we find ourselves feeling more confident and ready to handle any situation. Positive words encourage positive thinking, so add some "*I can…*" and "*I'm great*" phrases to your vocabulary! Positivity is contagious, so don't be afraid to share it with others and encourage them to think positive too.

Using positive language:

- Avoid negatives, such as "can't" or "won't"

- Reassure yourself and remind yourself of your abilities

- Compliment yourself – "*Good job*" and "*Well done*"

## Limit or Remove Negative Phrasing

As we've said before, positive words encourage positive thinking. The same goes for negative phrasing – when we allow ourselves to use negative language, our thoughts become negative. Studies have shown that there are five key phrases that any person should remove from their vocabulary in order to ban negative language.

- **Just** – This word limits our accomplishments and devalues our skills. By saying phrases such as "*I'm just an accountant*" or "*I just work in customer service*" can make anyone feel happy in their job.

- **Try** – This word can often give us an excuse to fail. We will 'try' to accomplish something, but if we don't succeed then it's not our fault. We either do something or we don't.

- **Can't** – This word is often used when a person does not want to take the effort to reach a goal or accomplishment. Replace this word with a mental action plan on how you can act on your goals.

- **Impossible** – This word is normally used when we are faced with something big and overwhelming. However, anything can seem possible if broken down into smaller, more attainable jobs. Anything can be accomplished when we take things one step at a time.

- **Someday**- This word can have the same problem as 'try' – it sets us up to allow failure. When we plan to reach our goals "someday", we are giving ourselves permission to procrastinate. Set a timeline for your goals and stick to them.

## Case Study

Stacy was angry that her manager had decided to give her another long project to complete.
*"Didn't he see how many mistakes I made last time?"* She became more frustrated when she felt like she did not have enough time to finish and would have to turn it in late. Stacy was ready to give up on the whole thing. When she spoke to her manager again, he told her that she always did a great job and that he had faith that she could complete this project successfully.

Stacy immediately began to feel better about it and decided to have a more positive outlook. She remembered the success she had on the last project and kept reminding herself she can do a great job. When she began to feel negative again, she just remembered her manager's words. When she turned in the final project, on time, she realized her critical thinking almost got the best of her.

# Chapter 4 – Four D Model

Appreciative inquiry opens whole new doors for us and opens our eyes to a new way of thinking. With positive thoughts and attitudes, we can discover new ways of reaching our goals. We can be free to dream new ambitions and set ourselves up for success. After a plan is made, we can design how to reach that goal and deliver the end result to us. Yes, we can accomplish all of this if we just believe that we have the skills and confidence to do it.

## Discovery

Discovery is about finding what type of processes, organization and skills work for you and will help you along your way. It is also a process of learning to appreciate what has been given to us and using it to our benefit. Employees often discover some of this information by speaking with other employees and learning about what has worked for the company in the past. This can lead employees to feel more appreciative about their role in the company and what they can do to make meaningful contributions.

Examples:

Conversing with other employees about their experiences

Asking managers what methods have worked in the past

Observing your past actions that have been successful

### Four D Model – Discovery Exercise

Discovery is the first step of the Four D Model. Make notes about 'discovering' what processes and plans work for your office. Makes notes as to why you think they have been successful so far.

## Dream

The dream phase focuses on what would work for yourself and the company in the future. This 'dream session' can be run in a large group conference or can be done with a few peers. Either way, it should allow everyone to open up about what they want to see from the company and any ideas they may have for improvement. The idea of the 'dream' part of this model is to use positive energy to create a vision for the future, while creating goals and accomplishments that will help you, and the company, reach that point. Dream up the ideal and perfect situation.

Examples:

- "Would this work in the future?"

- "What do I want to see happen?"

- "What would be perfect for me and the company?"

### Four D Model – Dream Exercise
Dream is the second step of the Four D Model. Make notes or comments regarding your professional dreams. What do you want to see happen? What do you hope will change?

## Design

The design plan is all about how you and the company plan to reach the goals and dreams that were lined out in the discovery and dream phases. This part of the model focuses on what needs to be done to reach these goals and reach the progress needed. Generally this part is carried out by a small group of members that concentrate on how to move forward, but it can be done with larger groups as well. Anyone in this group is encouraged to remember to use positive language and encourage their coworkers to think positive in their work.

Examples:

- "What do we need to do to make this happen?"

- "Will things needed to be changed or altered?"

- "Do we need to introduce a new element?"

### Four D Model – Design Exercise
Design is the third step of the Four D Model. Sketch out a plan design that you would use for your Discovery and Dream ideas. What do you need to include? What aspects do you need to cover?

## Delivery

The delivery phase, sometimes called the destiny phase, is the final stage of the Four D model, and focuses on executing the plans and ideas that were thought out and developed in the previous phases. In this part of the model, employees need to take the necessary actions to progress toward change and positively obtaining their goals. A plan isn't worth the paper it is written on if it doesn't have a dynamic team behind it to carry it out.

Examples:

- Implement any changes needed

- Remove elements that no longer work

- Assign tasks and duties as needed

### Four D Model – Delivery Exercise
Delivery is the final step of the Four D Model. Make or sketch a final plan on how you would delivery new ideas in the

office. What part do you play? What part do your coworkers play?

## Case Study

Jeremy was working with a group of employees who were working to create a new form of marketing for the company. Many of them had run out of ideas and weren't sure where to start. So Jeremy asked the employees what have they noticed has worked for the company in the past. Everyone named several methods that have been successful. Then he asked them what they wanted to see for the marketing scheme, whether it was successful or if it fell through.

He wanted them to imagine the big picture. Then he asked them to come up with one action that would get them to that success. He asked them what resources and items they would need to get there. When several employees displayed their new ideas, Jeremy told them the last thing they needed to do was put them into action. That was their next big step.

# Chapter 5 – Four I Model

The Four I Model is very similar to the Four D Model previously discussed; however, while the Four D Model focuses on the individual employee as well as a small group of employees, the Four I Model is designed to think one step above that. This model focuses on taking changes and plans designed by employees and implement them to other levels of the company, such as upper management and stakeholders.

## Initiate

In the initiate phase, people are introduced to the Appreciative Inquiry theory and how it can help in company. This phase is important to develop planning and strategies. It debuts new plans and ideas the employees have about the company and what can be improved upon (or even changed). These ideas are usually backed up with previous experiences, employee research and documented successes or failures. From this, upper management can begin to formulate a plan for themselves and what they can do to aid in the process.

Examples:

- "What plans have been laid out for the company?"

- "What is my role in this?"

- "What should we focus on first?"

### Four I Model – Initiate Exercise

Initiate is the first step of the Four I Model. Sketch out various new ideas you want to see happen in your company. Think of changes that can affect any department, not just your own.

# Inquire

The Inquire phase aims to help employees begin to form a plan or course of action to make the plans in the Initiate phase. Also called 'the interview' stage, this part of the plan involves a lot of communicating between employees, managers, and higher ups. People are urged to share their ideas and visions which can be used as valuable input. Much of this is done in groups, large or small, but don't forget to utilize personal, one-on-one interviews as well. Remember to encourage positive language and include positive thinking methods for everyone involved.

Examples:

- "What do I want to see happen?"

- "What do my coworkers want to see happen?"

- "What do we need to make changes in the company?"

### Four I Model – Inquire Exercise
Inquire is the second step of the Four I Model. Ask the questions you want answered regarding new ideas. Where are they directed to? How can you express them? Etc.

# Imagine

The Imagine part of the plan focuses on forming a route of action for all of the ideas and brainstorms previously collected. Its purpose is to determine what needs to be done and how it can be carried out. Once a stable vision has been designed, it can be shared with other employees to ensure their participation. Ensure that the plan is introduced with a positive attitude and outlook to encourage employees into the plan and make them feel more confident about moving forward. Whether done in small or large group, every employee should have a positive outlook about moving forward with any action plan.

Examples:

- "What common ideas and themes did we find?"

- "What do we need to change?"

- "What steps do we need to take now?"

### Four I Model – Imagine Exercise

Imagine is the third step of the Four I Model. Now that you know what you want to see in your office or company, 'imagine' the ways they can be done. What type of planning is needed? How would the final result look like?

## Innovate

Finally, using Appreciative Inquiry, the action plan can be put into place and carried out according to its design. Employees may be fearful or skeptical at first, but this is where the positive language and attitudes are put to the test. Every person has a role and should take the steps necessary to carry out their part of the plan. Remind employees of their abilities and praise them for their efforts during this transition. Confident and self-assured employees are needed to support any change in the company and are key to a smooth plan implementation.

Examples:

- Recognize what is needed to carry out the plan

- Reinforce the action plan and what it is designed to do

- Encourage employees as they carry out the plan

## Four I Model – Innovate Exercise

Innovate is the final step of the Four I Model. Determine an action plan for making changes in your company. Keep a positive outlook and determine what you can do to make these changes happen.

## Case Study

Jeremy arrives at the manager meeting and says his employees have come up with a great new marketing plan. First, he lays out the design of the plan and describes how it would need to be initiated. He described what would need to be done and what kind of results it could bring to the company. He answered any questions they had and listened to their ideas and opinions.

He reminded them that the purpose of the plan was to increase marketing and boost sales to the company. When the managers were satisfied with his answers, they decide to give the plan a try and put it into place. As soon as the responsibilities were delegated and everyone knew their role, they could get the plan under way.

# Chapter 6 – Appreciative Inquiry Interview Style

Many people associate interviews with fear and anxiety and will immediately break into a sweat when they are called into one. But the Appreciative Inquiry interview style helps to do away with those stereotypes. This type of interview style focuses on positive questions, enjoyable stories, and discovering how the potential employee can make an impact on the company, without using scare tactics or fear.

## Framing Positive Questions

When we ask questions to the interviewee, what kind of response are we expecting? If we ask questions that can come across as negative or critical, we can expect that kind of answer. But by using positive language to form more positive questions, we can not only put the other person at ease, but they will feel more confident about their abilities and be able to have a better interview. Use positive experiences to help the person realize their own skills and ambitions, while at the same time determining how they would work with the team and the company.

Example questions:

- "What was the best job you've had?"

- "What do you value most in a job?"

- "What do you like best about yourself?"

### Becoming More Positive Exercise

Before you can begin to form positive questions to ask at an interview, you must first become a more positive person yourself. Make goals for yourself in ways that you can build a more positive attitude. Define your goals, identify activities to help form these goals, and identify ways to execute these activities.

### Solicit Positive Stories

If you open an interview describing how the last employee suddenly quit and left a pile of work for everyone else to do, the interviewee does not have a very positive outlook on the company from the start. Instead, open the interview with a positive experience and describe positive events that have happened. When using positive questions, have the interviewee share their positive experiences and personal qualities. When a person can share openly about a happy situation or personal experience, they feel more at ease and are more prone to being positive themselves, which can mean good news for the company as a new employee.

## Finding What Works

When we interview an employee, we already have an idea of the qualities and skills needed for the position. We know what it takes when working for the company and what qualities should be possessed by the employee. However, there is always more than one way to utilize these skills and put them to good use. The key is to find out what works for the company as well as the employee. Do they work better based on experience? Do they have positive energy to contribute? Do they have a positive outlook? When you find that happy medium between the two, you'll find a great fit for everyone.

### Finding Out What Works Exercise

As one of the hiring personnel, you know what you are looking for in an applicant. Write down key qualities you find in applicants and how they can work for the company.

## Recognize the Reoccurring Themes

When interviewing and sharing stories with someone, recognize the reoccurring themes that each person shares. Look for a pattern in what they have experienced and achieved and what they have in common. Some of the common themes you may hear include commitment, expertise, trust, etc. When you recognize the reoccurring themes, you can decide together which one, or ones, are the most important and which ones you favor the most for the company. With these themes, you can build a plan together because you will know what each of you value and exactly what you will want from the experience.

Common reoccurring themes in interviews:

- Commitment – Seeing a project through to the end

- Loyalty – Staying even when the going gets tough

- Experience – Valuable on many levels

- Cohesion – Teamwork and being a team player

## Case Study

Debra was interviewing an employee that has been with the company for a number of years. She could tell he was a little nervous, but she wasn't sure how to make him feel more at ease. After speaking with him for a while, she asks him what his favorite task that he'd had so far. She noticed how excited he became and began to describe a time when he and his collogues worked together and solved a challenging manufacturing problem.

She encouraged him to share his stories, noticing how comfortable he was feeling now. She asked him to pull out the positive characteristics of his other tasks and did he see a pattern emerge. Debra noticed he had similar qualities in all of his work and that he had a good skill set from them. Before he left, she thanked him for sharing his experiences and was glad to see him finally smiling.

# Chapter 7 – Anticipatory Reality

Anticipatory reality is helpful in appreciative inquiry because it makes us focus on the future and what we want. One of the first steps of anticipatory reality is creating an image of the future and determining what can help you get there. We can change things, add new themes, and make goals – we are constantly fashioning our anticipatory reality.

## Imagining a Successful Future Will Affect the Present

We know that our past does not always identify our future. But planning our future can affect our present. Thinking ahead to our successful future can increase our positivity in our lives today and raise our confidence. When we focus on the successes we want to achieve and imagine them coming true, it can give us great hope for the future, which in turn gives us hope for today. We can stay positive by knowing that we can achieve that successful future and always keep a positive attitude about reaching our goals.

Benefits:

- Positive outlook

- Goal successes

- Improved focus

### Planning Your Future Now Exercise

In order to plan for a successful future, you must first make goals that you can work to achieve. Outline your career and personal goals and what you hope to accomplish. Identify your career goals and personal goals.

## Controlling Negative Anticipation

Many of us are the type of people who automatically assume the worst in any situation. We start to anticipate anything that can go wrong and try to determine how we would handle anything that comes up. But if we learn to control these negative anticipations, we can begin to see any situation from the positive side. When we view the positive aspects of a situation, we feel more confident about our ability to handle them. Because no matter how big or scary a situation may seem, remaining positive and changing how we view the problem can make anything possible.

Example:

- Watch for hidden negative thoughts or assumptions

- Avoid jumping to conclusions

- Realize the problem is in the situation – not you

### Limit your Negative Anticipation Exercise

List some situation that cause you to have negative anticipations (going to the doctor, working in a group, etc.) Think of ways you could think more positively about it.

## Current Decisions Will Be Influenced Positively

The decisions we make today can influence how we see things later. When we limit our negative anticipations and concentrate on creating a positive outlook, our current decisions and thoughts begin to develop into a positive form of thinking, which can improve our overall confidence. Worrying about what may or may not happen or what could go wrong in a situation can drain our bodies and make us feel as though we don't have any hope. But if we change our thoughts today and limit the negativity we allow in our planning, our decisions can be influenced by positivity and will help us make better choices in our everyday lives.

Benefits:

- More confidence in your decisions

- Less negative or anxious feelings

- Positive outlook on future decisions

## Base It on Data and Real Examples

One of the negative things about anticipatory reality is that we often base our thoughts and conclusions on things that we have heard or have over-played in our own heads. We begin to think about the worst thing that could happen or anything that could go wrong, but we have nothing to base it upon. Instead, we should always focus on the facts of a problem and realize what is actually there.

For example: you forgot to turn in a weekly report to your manager. Part of you begins to panic and starts thinking of the negative possibilities that could come from it, such as employee demerits, upsetting your boss or even getting fired. But when you stop to look at the facts and data that are involved in this situation, we can remain calm and positive. We know that (in this instance), the manager allows reports to be turned in a day late with a reasonable explanation. He has told you before that if something comes up, you are free to go speak with him. Once you've reviewed this helpful piece of information to yourself, you feel less worried about the little mistake you make and feel more confident about picking yourself back up and moving on.

Avoid:

- "Word of mouth" stories

- The "maybe" or "what if" possibilities

- Dramatized outcomes or over-reactions

### Basing Things on Fact or Data Exercise

List some situations that cause us to jump to conclusions or make assumptions and think of a way we can fix these assumptions by focusing on facts or real data.

## Case Study

Bruce was finishing his report on the new accounting software and was preparing to show it to his manager. He wanted to believe the manager would like it and would credit the employees working with the software. But he wasn't really sure how it would go over with him. He began to doubt himself and doubt if the software was fit for the company. He became worried that the manager would overlook his numbers and make decisions that didn't benefit anyone. Bruce then realized he was over reacting and needed to show the report first. He told himself to think positively now and wait to see what the manager thought. When the manager complimented his report findings and the use of the software, Bruce knew he had over thought his reaction too much.

# Chapter 8 – The Power of Positive Imagery

Imagery can be seen in a variety of ways. It helps us to create a full picture of an idea or situation based on details and facts that we're presented with. Positive imagery is a key tool in helping us to remain positive and have an upbeat look on any problem. The key is to find what imagery works for you and using it to help you accomplish your goals and ambitions.

## Shaping Performance with Positive Imagery

Positive imagery can often serve as not only a reminder of good work, but it can also serve as a reward. You should be seeing an increase in performance and productivity through the use of positive imagery. Some physical forms of positive imagery include a shiny trophy after a race or a chart of how many products you sold last month. But we can also have mental positive imagery that can help us along our way when we cannot see our physical rewards.

Our performance is based upon the kind of outcome we want, and if we reinforce what we want with positive imagery, then we are not afraid to go after it. Maybe it's the image of having happy coworkers when you complete a project or the image of an empty desk at the end of the week. Remind yourself of these positive images to keep you focused on the task at hand and doing your best to get it done.

### Keeping Positive Imagery Exercise

Positive Imagery comes in many forms, including physical symbols or emotional ones. Write what type of positive imagery you keep around or think about to make yourself feel more positive. What things do you keep at home? What things do you keep at work?

## Being Better Prepared for Adversity

Being positive does not mean that you are oblivious to the outside world and the things that can go wrong in it. But, being positive does mean that you can be prepared for the worst but keeping a positive outlook for everything else. Being prepared for adversity simply means that you do not lie to yourself about what can happen and that you see the situation for what it is. You know that things can be different and will change, but you don't let it damper your outlook. When you are better prepared, you have the knowledge to know that you may not be able to change the world and the problems that arise in it, but you can change your own life and have the choice to remain positive while dealing with any negative situation.

## People are More Flexible and Creative

When a problem is presented before you, chances are, you cannot change what has already happened or the effect of the problem on everyone else. But you as a person are more flexible and creative and have the ability to manipulate how you view a problem and how to solve it. Realize that you have options and that you can control how you react to something. Don't look at the problem as though it only has a black or white solution – remember there is a gray area too and you will find the best way for you to handle it.

Remember:

- You can change even if the problem can't.

- You can control only you.

- There is more than one correct way to do things.

# Think of the Perfect Situation

When we see something as perfect, we generally see something that is free of flaws and makes us happy. Sometimes when we have a large group of problems, we have trouble deciding what to start on first. When this happens, a helpful exercise is to think about the perfect situation. When you do, what is the first problem you notice is missing? Not only does it help you determine which problem you should tackle first, but it lets you have an image of a perfect situation without the problem, so you know it is not impossible! Visualizing the perfect situation can help propel you in direction needed to remedy almost any situation.

- What is a perfect situation?

- What makes the situation perfect?

- What problem(s) instantly go away?

- Can you do it on your own? Will you need help?

### The Perfect Situation Exercise
Outline what you would consider a perfect situation. What problems is missing that makes it perfect? What can you do to reach that perfect situation?

# Case Study

Anna was working on a design project for the new library that was opening soon. After hours of tedious work, she felt as though she wouldn't finish on time or have enough energy to make a great design. She began to feel discouraged and depressed. When she walked back into her office, she saw the small plaque she received after her last design project. It made her smile to remember that she had done something so successful.

She remembered the problems she had on the last project and thought about how she dealt with them. Anna knew this project was different and had more steps to it than the last one, but she knew how to handle those when they came up. When she thought of her finished design, she thought of how great the library would look and how it would benefit so many people. Feeling more confident and positive, Anna set back to work on her design.

# Chapter 9 – Influencing Change Through Appreciative Inquiry

Influencing other people can have a ripple effect – it can start small but then the efforts begin to grow and grow. Of course we want to influence other people in a positive manner, not a negative one. Through Appreciative Inquiry, we can influence others by not only being positive ourselves, but helping other people make changes in their lives and be a more positive person too.

## Using Strengths to Solve Challenges

Every problem or challenge is different. Some of them we can handle on our own. Some of them require help from others. Whatever the case, we know that we can solve the problem the best way we know how by using our inner strengths. Maybe you think well when you look at the big picture or you take a step-by-step approach toward any solution.

The key is to find what your strength is and use it to your advantage. Use Appreciative Inquiry to ask yourself what kind of strengths have worked for you before. Ask yourself how you felt when you used them to solve a problem and remember how confident you felt afterwards. These Appreciative Inquiry exercises will help you get to the root of your problem and then help you determine how to solve it!

### Identifying my Strengths Exercise

Make a list of your personal strengths and how they help you solve problems. Do not forget to look at all facets of your life to find your strengths. What strengths do you bring to your work, family, community, or volunteer activities? What do you like to do? What are you an expert in?

# Confidence Will Promote Positive Change

The perception you have of yourself not only affects how other people see you, but it can affect how you view the world and act in it. Sometimes we can't control these things, such as embarrassing moments or recent mistakes, but there are many things we can do that can boost our confidence. When we remember our earlier successes or imagine a goal we want to achieve, we get an instant confidence boost and can feel better about the choices we make. When we are confident in ourselves, we are more apt to make positive changes without being fearful and without our own criticism.

Tips to build confidence:

- Dress nicely.

- Present confidence body language.

- Offer you opinion and insights.

- Compliment other people – it makes you feel good too!

## My Confidence Exercise

Take a few minutes think about how you feel confident. Think of areas you feel most confident in and why. Then note areas in which you could be more confident, and why. What areas are you confident about? What areas do you wish you were more confident?

# Inquiry is a Seed of Change

Many things in our lives have changed so much and continue to grow over time. But what makes them change? What steps do they take to make something different? We'd be surprised to know that the simplest way to make changes is to ask a question. Inquiry is the seed of change because it brings up the mental question of "what if?"

- *"What if cell phones didn't just make calls, but sent a message of typed text?"*

- *"What if we sold fries with our hamburger and called it a combo meal?"*

- *"What if new customers received a 10% discount when they sign with us?"*

Through Appreciative Inquiry, anyone can ask a question that seeks to find another type of thinking. When different types of 'thinkers' come together, it can create various types of changes that can alter how we view many things in our lives.

## People Will Gravitate Towards What is Expected of Them

When you look for a job opening in the want ads, what type of ads do you notice first? Chances are you read the ones that mention your type of skill set, such as a secretary, a chef, or even a construction worker. You feel confident reading these ads first because you know that they are in your area of skills and you're confident you can do the job.

The same effect is true for anyone else. When people have an idea of what is expected of them, they are more likely to drift toward that persona. If we are positive and helpful in our own actions, people will naturally want to join in when we encourage them to feel the same way. They feel as though they are expected to feel more positive, upbeat or confident, so they begin to review how they do things and 'gravitate' towards a different way of doing things.

## Case Study

Allen was having trouble with solving a problem in the company's budget plan. He was feeling stumped and didn't know he could find a solution. He took a few minutes to remember his strengths, such as complex math skills and attention to detail. He kept reminding himself of his skills and began to feel confident in his ability to finish the problem. Feeling more confident, he was able to dig deeper into the budget and see if anything was out of the ordinary. He had solved a similar problem before, so he knew he could be the one to find the issue. After several more attempts, he found an error in the report that was causing him to come up short. Relieved at what he had found, Allen wondered why he doubted himself in the first place.

# Chapter 10 – Coaching and Managing with Appreciative Inquiry

Managing a group of people can be a difficult task by itself, much less trying to coach them in the right direction. Sometimes our good intentions can come across as critical, negative, or just plain mean. But when we use Appreciative Inquiry along with other coaching or management strategies, we can help our employees find a solution to their problems while also making them more positive and confident in themselves.

## Build Around What Works

When we examine how our business is run, we notice what functions and works for everyone, and what doesn't. The key to a well-managed team is building around what works and encouraging growth with it. As managers or leaders we can try to change things that derail our employees from what they usually do. While this is normally done with good intentions, it can often lead to a kink in the company plan and actually have the opposite effect of what we were hoping for. Notice what is working for the employees now and how well they function. If changes are needed (or attempted), try to incorporate the current structure while leading the employees in the new direction.

Like the old saying goes: *"If it isn't broke, don't fix it."*

### Building Around What Works Exercise

As a manager or leader, we know what works for our employees and what gives them the confidence they need. Outline some things you noticed that work for your employees. Then note ways you can keep them feeling confident while doing it.

## Focus on Increases

As a leader, we often look at our task list in a negative way. One of the first things we try to accomplish is to decrease certain areas, such as mistakes, tardiness, and complaints. But focusing on what we want to decrease normally includes negative attributes of the job. If we focus on these things for too long, we can drive ourselves to negativity very quickly.

Instead, focus on what aspects can be increased. By focusing on what can be increased, we are focusing on positive attributes of the job, such as more sales, more goals, and more customer and employee satisfaction. If we approached an employee with the same problem, which route of improvement would they feel more confident taking – decreasing their typing mistakes or increasing their typing ability?

Encourage increases in different areas:

- Sales

- Moral

- Productivity

- Confidence

### Focusing on Increases Exercise

Note areas you want to increase in your job. Avoid using negative words or phrases. Start with the phrase "I want to increase…" and fill in the blank.

## Recognize the Best in People

Another aspect of being positive is being able to see the best in people instead of being critical. Of course no one is perfect and everyone has some kind of fault, but that does mean we have to define them by it. When we recognize the best in people, not only do we benefit from knowing what great attributes they can contribute, but it makes the employees feel more confident about themselves and their job skills.

When they feel better about themselves, they want to do better at their job and will work harder to make progress and get the job done. Don't be afraid to compliment employees on their job skills and what they have accomplished. When you find yourself focusing on what they have done wrong, refer to your mental list of all of their good qualities and determine which list overpowers the other.

## Limit or Remove Negative Comments

Using negative terms and phrases is one of the leading causes of poor performance and low employee morale. These harsh words can damage any employee relationship and can often bring out a sense of defensiveness when approached. When you find yourself wanting to use negative phrases, either with yourself or an employee, stop and think of the words you're using. Then rethink the sentence by removing negative comments and replacing them with a positive one. You'll find that you can still get your point across without making the employee feel as though they are being attacked.

Remove comments such as:

- "It's too hard."

- "I'll/You'll never finish this."

- "It's too late to change now."

## Case Study

Michelle is managing group of new hires in the medical records department. To help introduce them to the different processes and tasks they used in the department, she detailed what the other employees used, since it was most effective and made minimal mistakes. She didn't want to offend the new employees, so instead of telling them what to stay away from, she reminded them of things they can improve on, such as filing speed, or their attention to detail. Although she knew these employees were new to the department, she could tell most of them had the right skills. She continued to work with them as they became more familiar with the way of doing things and stayed nearby in case they had any questions.

# Chapter 11 – Creating a Positive Core

If we want others around us to be positive and confident, then we have to create it within ourselves first. This can mean first focusing on yourself and your positive core and then creating a positive core among your employees. Building a strong core in yourself ensures that you can have the confidence you need to complete any job. Having a strong, positive core among employees ensures that coworkers can work together and still maintain their own confidence. A strong core can stick together despite rough problems that may arise.

## Strengths

Identifying our strengths can give us an instant confidence boost because it reminds ourselves of things we can do that are really great. But sometimes when we don't notice our strengths right away, we assume that we don't have any, or worse, downplay the ones we do have. A common exercise to find our strengths includes making a list of everything that we are good at. Review this list several times and remember a time when you had to use each attribute. Keep this list nearby to always remind yourself of them and remain confident.

Tips for finding strengths:

- Analyze how you handle situations

- Determine what your desires are and how you go after them

- Examine the ways you solve problems

## Best Practices

Sometime the term 'best practices' can seem confusing if we don't attach them to something. In Appreciative Inquiry, best practices refer to the practices that work best for you and what work best for the company. What practices make you the most confident and positive? What practices make you feel successful when you finish them? What practices improve employee morale and progress? Remember that these practices can be individualized to each person, so what works for one person may not work for another.

Tips:

- What practices make you feel as though you've accomplished something?

- What practices boost your confidence?

- What practices make you feel positive about the end result?

## Peak Experiences

Peak experiences are commonly defined as moments in which we feel the highest levels of happiness and possibility. They can happen in everyday situations or during extreme events in our lives. They can happen when we accomplish a new goal or finish a long project. The key is to remember how they made us feel and made us feel positive and confident. While they are not necessarily an 'ah-ha' moment in our lives, peak experiences can help us notice key moments in our lives and how we felt when we experienced them. Keeping these memories with you at all times will ensure that you can always receive a lift of positivity when we need it.

### My Peak Experiences Exercise

Write down some of your peak experiences you've had in life. Describe where you were, how you felt, and what happened after it occurred.

# Successes

Sometimes personal modesty can keep us from seeing our own successes, which can keep us from feeling fully confident or self-assured. Our past successes are often viewed as our roots, or the areas that be started from and built upon to progress forward. We often forget to use these successes to remind us what it took to get us to our personal level of achievements. But when we relive these successes, it can remind us that we can overcome almost anything and can feel ultimately better about ourselves. When we feel more confident in ourselves and our success, it can reduce our stress and serves as an anchor for positivity.

Remembering successes:

- Keep a visual reminder, such as a trophy or chart.

- Review these successes in your head constantly

- Talk about successes with friends and learn from each other

### My Successes Exercise

Write down some of your personal successes you've had in life. Describe where you were, how you felt, and what happened after it occurred.

# Case Study

Robert was feeling depressed after his last presentation. He felt as though he didn't do as great of a job as he normally does and was feeling sad about it. Robert was determined to bounce back on his next presentation. First, he made a list of all of his personal strengths and how he puts them to good use. Then he made notes of some ways his strengths helped him reach his other goals. When he remembered all of his past successes, he felt very confident in himself and felt like he could do a better job on the next project. He was determined not to let one mishap stop him from succeeding next time.

## Additional Titles

The 90 Minute Guide series of books covers a variety of general business skills and are intended to be completed in 90 minutes or less. It is an effective way for building your skill set and can be used to acquire professional development units needed by project managers and other industries to maintain their certification. For the availability of titles please see www.silvercitypublications.com/shop/.

No. 1 - Appreciative Inquiry

No. 2 - Assertiveness and Self Control

No. 3 - Attention Management

No. 4 - Body Language Basics

No. 5 - Business Acumen

No. 6 - Business and Etiquette

No. 7 - Change Management

No. 8 - Coaching and Mentoring

No. 9 - Communications Strategies

No. 10 - Conflict Resolution

No. 11 - Creative Problem Solving

No. 12 - Delivering Constructive Criticism

No. 13 - Developing Creativity

No. 14 - Developing Emotional Intelligence

No. 15 - Developing Interpersonal Skills

No. 16 - Developing Social Intelligence

No. 17 - Employee Motivation

No. 18 - Facilitation Skills

No. 19 - Goal Setting and Getting Things Done

No. 20 - Knowledge Management Fundamentals

No. 21 - Leadership and Influence

No. 22 - Lean Process and Six Sigma Basics

No. 23 - Managing Anger

No. 24 - Meeting Management

No. 25 - Negotiation Skills

No. 26 - Networking Inside a Company

No. 27 - Networking Outside a Company

No. 28 - Office Politics for Managers

No. 29 - Organizational Skills

No. 30 - Performance Management

No. 31 - Presentation Skills

No. 32 - Public Speaking

No. 33 - Servant Leadership

No. 34 - Team Building for Management

No. 35 - Team Work and Team Building

No. 36 - Time Management

No. 37 - Top 10 Soft Skills You Need

No. 38 - Virtual Team Building and Management

www.ingramcontent.com/pod-product-compliance
Lightning Source LLC
Chambersburg PA
CBHW060625030426
42337CB00018B/3198